ALEX MORGAN

From Playground to World Cup (A Biography Book for Kids)

Harry Howze

Copyright @ 2024 By Harry Howze

All rights reserved. No part of this book may be reproduced, distributed, or transmitted in any form or by any means, including photocopying, recording, or other electronic or mechanical methods, without the prior written permission of the publisher, except in the case of brief quotations embodied in critical reviews and specific other noncommercial uses permitted by copyright law.

Disclaimer

The following book is for entertainment and informational purposes only, for children. The information presented is without contract or any type of guarantee assurance. While every caution has been taken to provide accurate and current information, it is solely the reader's responsibility to check all information contained in this article before relying upon it. Neither the author nor the publisher can be held accountable for any errors or omissions.

Under no circumstances will any legal responsibility or blame be held against the author or publisher for any reparation, damages, or monetary loss due to the information presented, either directly or indirectly. This book is not intended as legal or medical advice. If any such specialized advice is needed, seek a qualified individual for help.

Trademarks are used without permission. Use of the trademark is not authorized by, associated with, or sponsored by the trademark owners. All trademarks and brands used within this book are used with no intent to infringe on the trademark owners and are only used for clarifying purposes.

This book is not sponsored by or affiliated with soccer, its teams, the players, or anyone involved with them.

Table Of Contents

INTRODUCTION

CHAPTER 1: LITTLE ALEX'S BIG DREAMS

CHAPTER 2: KICKIN' IT IN HIGH SCHOOL

CHAPTER 3: COLLEGE GOALS: ON AND OFF THE FIELD

CHAPTER 4: JOINING TEAM USA: A DREAM COME TRUE

CHAPTER 5: OLYMPIC GLORY: LONDON 2012

CHAPTER 6: WORLD CUP WONDER: CANADA 2015

CHAPTER 7: SUPER STRIKER: ALEX'S PLAYING STYLE

CHAPTER 8: MORE THAN JUST GOALS

CHAPTER 9: THE JOURNEY CONTINUES

CONCLUSION

INTRODUCTION

Welcome, young readers!

Have you ever dreamed of becoming a sports superstar? Of hearing thousands of fans cheer your name? Of holding a shiny gold medal in your hands? If so, you're about to meet someone very special who turned those exact dreams into reality!

This is the story of Alex Morgan, one of the world's greatest soccer players.

But guess what? Alex wasn't always a famous athlete. She was once a kid just like you, with big dreams and a love for kicking a ball around.

In this book, we'll go on an exciting journey with Alex. We'll start on the playgrounds where she first fell in love with soccer, and end up at the World Cup, where she became a champion! Along the way, you'll discover how Alex's hard work, determination, and never-give-up attitude helped her overcome challenges and reach for the stars.

So, are you ready to lace up your sneakers and join Alex on her incredible adventure? Who knows, her story might just inspire you to chase your own dreams, whether they're on a soccer field or anywhere else in the world!

Let's get started! The crowd is cheering, the whistle is about to blow, and Alex Morgan's amazing story is waiting for you on the next page.

Come on, let's go!

CHAPTER 1: LITTLE ALEX'S BIG DREAMS

Imagine a sunny day in Diamond Bar, California. A little girl with bouncy pigtails and a big smile is running around her backyard, kicking a soccer ball. This is Alex Morgan, and she's having the time of her life!

Alex wasn't always the soccer superstar we know today. Once upon a time, she was just a kid who loved to play. Her dad, Michael, introduced her to soccer when she was barely old enough to walk. From that moment on, Alex was hooked!

On the playground, Alex was always the first to suggest a game of soccer. She'd gather her friends, set up makeshift goals using jackets or backpacks, and play for hours. Her eyes would light up every time she scored a goal, and she'd jump up and down with excitement.

But it wasn't always easy. Sometimes, the older kids didn't want to let her play because she was younger or because she was a girl. Did that stop Alex? No way! She'd practice even harder, showing everyone that she could keep up with the best of them.

At home, Alex would spend hours in her backyard, dribbling the ball between trees and shooting at a goal her dad set up for her. She'd imagine she was playing in a big stadium, with thousands of fans cheering her on. Little did she know that one day, those daydreams would come true!

Alex's family was always there to support her. Her mom, Pamela, would bring orange slices to her games, and her sisters, Jeni and Jeri, would cheer her on from the sidelines. They could see the sparkle in Alex's eyes whenever she played soccer, and they knew this was more than just a game to her.

As Alex grew, so did her dreams. She started to watch professional soccer games on TV and dreamed of playing just like her heroes. She'd practice their moves in her backyard, imagining herself scoring the winning goal in a World Cup final.

Little Alex may have been small, but her dreams were enormous. And the best part? She was just getting started on her incredible journey. The playground was her first stadium, and every kick of the ball was taking her one step closer to her goals.

Remember, every big dream starts somewhere. For Alex Morgan, it all began in her backyard and on the playground. Where will your dreams begin?

CHAPTER 2: KICKIN' IT IN HIGH SCHOOL

Welcome to Diamond Bar High School! The halls are buzzing with chatter, but all eyes are on a tall, athletic girl striding confidently down the corridor. That's our Alex, and she's not just any high school student – she's about to become a soccer sensation!

Alex joined the Brahmas, her high school soccer team, and boy, did she make an entrance! From her very first game, it was clear that this girl had something special. She zipped across the field like lightning, leaving defenders dizzy and goalkeepers scratching their heads.

But being a star player wasn't always a walk in the park. Alex had to juggle her time between soccer practice, homework, and hanging out with friends. Sometimes, she'd be so tired after a tough game that she'd fall asleep with her cleats still on! But Alex knew that to achieve her dreams, she had to work hard both on and off the field.

In class, Alex wasn't just doodling soccer balls in her notebook (okay, maybe sometimes she was). She worked hard to keep her grades up, knowing that being a good student was just as important as being a good athlete. Her teachers were impressed by her dedication – she attacked her studies with the same energy she showed on the soccer field!

Alex's high school years weren't all about soccer, though. She made great friends, went to school dances, and even tried other sports like track and volleyball. But nothing could compare to the thrill she felt when she was on the soccer field.

As the goals started piling up, people began to take notice. Newspapers wrote about the "goal-scoring machine" from Diamond Bar High. College scouts started showing up at her games. Alex was becoming a local celebrity!

But fame didn't change Alex. She remained the same friendly, determined girl who always had time to sign an autograph for a young fan or help a teammate with their technique. She knew that being a good person was just as important as being a good player.

By the time Alex was a senior, she had scored an incredible 106 goals in her high school career! She was named an All-American and earned a spot on the U.S. under-20 women's national team. High school was coming to an end, but for Alex, it was just the beginning of an amazing journey.

As Alex tossed her graduation cap in the air, she knew that all her hard work in high school – both in class and on the field – had set her up for an exciting future. The next challenge? College soccer! But that's a story for our next chapter...

Remember, whether you're on the field or in the classroom, giving your best effort can lead to amazing things. Just ask Alex Morgan!

CHAPTER 3: COLLEGE GOALS: ON AND OFF THE FIELD

Imagine stepping onto a huge college campus for the first time. That's exactly what Alex did when she arrived at the University of California, Berkeley. With her soccer cleats in one hand and textbooks in the other, Alex was ready for a whole new adventure!

At UC Berkeley, Alex joined the Golden Bears soccer team. But college soccer was a whole different ball game! The players were bigger, faster, and stronger than in high school. Did this scare Alex? No way! She saw it as a chance to push herself even harder.

Alex's freshman year was like riding a roller coaster. There were ups, like scoring her first college goal (and boy, was that exciting!), and downs, like getting injured and having to sit out some games. But Alex didn't let setbacks keep her down. She used her time off the field to study harder and cheer on her teammates.

In class, Alex discovered she had a knack for political economy. It might sound complicated, but to Alex, it was like planning a game strategy – figuring out how different parts work together. She'd often be found in the library, nose buried in books, working just as hard on her studies as she did on her soccer skills.

As the years went by, Alex became a star player for the Golden Bears. She led her team in scoring and was even named to the All-Pac-10 first team. But Alex's biggest college moment came when she wasn't even at college!

In 2008, during her junior year, Alex got a call that changed everything. She was invited to play for the U.S. Under-20 Women's National Team in the FIFA U-20 Women's World Cup!

Imagine representing your country while still in college!

Alex scored an amazing goal in the championship game, helping the U.S. team win the tournament. It was like something out of a movie – the crowd cheering, teammates hugging, and Alex realizing that her childhood dreams were coming true.

Back at Berkeley, Alex had to work extra hard to catch up on her studies. But she showed that with determination and good time management, you can chase your dreams and still hit the books.

By the time Alex graduated in 2010, she had scored 45 goals in her college career, ranking third all-time for UC Berkeley. But more importantly, she left with a degree, lifelong friends, and the skills to take on the world – both on and off the soccer field.

As Alex tossed her graduation cap in the air for the second time, she knew that college had prepared her for the next big step: becoming a professional soccer player. But how did she make the leap from college star to Team USA superstar? Well, that's coming up in our next exciting chapter!

Remember, just like Alex, you can score goals in sports and in your studies. It's all about giving your best shot in everything you do!

CHAPTER 4: JOINING TEAM USA: A DREAM COME TRUE

Close your eyes and picture this: You're standing in a locker room, heart pounding, as you slip on a jersey with the letters "USA" across the chest. For Alex Morgan, this wasn't just a daydream – it was about to become her reality!

In 2010, just after finishing college, Alex got the call she'd been dreaming of since she was a little girl kicking a ball around her backyard. She was invited to join the senior U.S. Women's National Team! Can you imagine how excited she must have been?

Alex's first game with Team USA was against Mexico. As she stepped onto the field, her knees were shaking a little. These weren't just any players – they were the best of the best! But as soon as the whistle blew, Alex's nerves disappeared. She was right where she belonged.

Being the newest and youngest player on the team wasn't always easy. Alex had to work extra hard to prove herself. She'd stay late after practice, perfecting her shots and working on her speed. Her teammates started calling her "Baby Horse" because of how fast she could run!

Alex's big breakthrough came in a game against Italy. The U.S. team needed to win to qualify for the World Cup, and the score was tied. In the final minutes, Alex scored the winning goal! The crowd went wild, her teammates hugged her, and Alex realized she wasn't just part of the team – she was making a real difference.

But it wasn't all about scoring goals. Alex learned so much from her teammates. Players like Abby

Wambach and Megan Rapinoe became like big sisters to her, teaching her tricks of the trade and showing her what it means to be a true team player.

Off the field, Alex had to get used to a whole new lifestyle. There were interviews to do, fans asking for autographs, and lots of traveling. It was exciting but sometimes overwhelming. Alex missed her family and friends back home, but she knew she was living her dream.

As Alex settled into her role on Team USA, she set new goals for herself. She wanted to play in the Olympics, win a World Cup, and inspire young girls to follow their dreams, just like she had.

With every game, every goal, and every cheer from the crowd, Alex's confidence grew. She wasn't just Alex Morgan from Diamond Bar anymore – she was Alex Morgan, star forward for the U.S. Women's National Team!

As the team prepared for the upcoming Olympics, Alex knew that the biggest challenges – and the biggest opportunities – were still ahead. But she was ready. After all, she had been preparing for this moment her entire life.

Remember, when you work hard and believe in yourself, amazing things can happen. Just ask Alex Morgan, the girl who went from dreaming about Team USA to wearing its jersey!

CHAPTER 5: OLYMPIC GLORY: LONDON 2012

Picture a massive stadium filled with thousands of cheering fans, flags waving from every country, and the biggest sports stars in the world all in one place. Welcome to the London 2012 Olympics, where Alex Morgan was about to make her Olympic debut!

As Alex walked into the Olympic Village for the first time, her eyes were as big as saucers. Everywhere she looked, there were world-class athletes from different sports and countries. It was like a dream come true – she was now an Olympian!

The U.S. Women's Soccer team was determined to win gold, and Alex was ready to give it her all. In their very first game against France, things didn't start well. The U.S. was down 2-0. But Alex and her teammates didn't give up. They fought back hard, and guess who scored the final goal to seal their 4-2 victory? That's right – Alex Morgan!

As the tournament went on, Alex proved she wasn't just a substitute player anymore. She was a key part of the team, scoring goals and setting up her teammates. In a nail-biting semifinal against Canada, Alex scored the winning goal in the last minute of extra time. Can you imagine how that felt? The whole team piled on top of her in celebration!

Then came the big day – the gold medal match against Japan. The stadium was packed, and millions of people were watching on TV back home. Alex's family was in the stands, wearing shirts with her number and waving American flags.

The game was intense, with both teams fighting hard. Alex assisted in one of the goals, helping the U.S.

team secure a 2-1 victory. When the final whistle blew, Alex and her teammates erupted in joy. They had done it – they were Olympic champions!

Standing on the podium, with the gold medal around her neck and the national anthem playing, Alex felt a rush of emotions. She thought about all the hard work, all the practices, all the times she'd dreamed of this moment as a little girl. And now, here she was, an Olympic gold medalist!

After the Olympics, Alex returned home to a hero's welcome. People recognized her on the street, kids asked for her autograph, and she even got to meet the President! But even with all this excitement, Alex knew that this was just the beginning. She had achieved one dream, but she had many more to chase.

As Alex looked at her gold medal, she realized something important. It wasn't just a piece of metal – it was a symbol of what you can achieve when you work hard, believe in yourself, and never give up on your dreams.

Remember, every big victory is made up of many small efforts. Alex's Olympic glory didn't happen overnight – it was the result of years of dedication and perseverance. So whatever your dream is, keep working at it. You never know, you might end up with a gold medal of your own one day!

CHAPTER 6: WORLD CUP WONDER: CANADA 2015

Imagine the excitement of the Olympics, but even bigger – that's the FIFA Women's World Cup! In 2015, Alex and her teammates headed to Canada, ready to take on the world's best soccer teams. The energy was electric, and Alex could feel the butterflies in her stomach. This was the moment she'd been working towards her entire life!

The tournament started with a bang for Team USA. In their very first game against Australia, Alex assisted in a goal that helped secure a 3-1 victory. But it wasn't all smooth sailing. The team faced tough opponents and nail-biting moments. In one game against Colombia, Alex got injured and had to sit out. It was hard for her to watch from the sidelines, but she cheered her teammates on with all her heart.

As the tournament progressed, the pressure grew. Every game was do-or-die. Alex pushed through her injury, determined to help her team however she could. In the semifinal against Germany, she drew a crucial penalty that helped the USA win 2-0. The team was headed to the final!

The night before the championship game against Japan, Alex could hardly sleep. She thought about all the early morning practices, the tough losses, and the sweet victories that had led to this moment. She was ready to give it her all.

On July 5, 2015, Alex stepped onto the field for the World Cup final. The stadium was a sea of red, white, and blue as American fans cheered. The game was intense, but Team USA came out strong. Alex's teammate Carli Lloyd scored an amazing hat-trick, and the team secured a 5-2 victory. They had done it – they were World Cup champions!

As the final whistle blew, Alex and her teammates erupted in joyous celebration. They hugged, cried, and laughed together. Alex looked up into the stands and saw her family cheering, their faces beaming with pride. She had dreamed of this moment since she was a little girl, and now it was real!

During the medal ceremony, as the golden trophy was passed around, Alex held it high above her head. The weight of the trophy reminded her of all the hard work, sweat, and tears that had gone into this victory. It wasn't just her triumph – it was a win for her team, her country, and all the young soccer players watching at home.

After the World Cup, Alex and her teammates returned to the USA as heroes. There were parades, TV appearances, and even a ticker-tape celebration in New York City! But for Alex, the best part was seeing young girls at soccer fields across the country, wearing jerseys with her name on the back. She realized that she wasn't just living her own dream – she was inspiring others to chase theirs too.

As the excitement of the World Cup victory settled, Alex knew that this was just another step in her journey. There would be more challenges ahead, more goals to score, and more dreams to chase. But for now, she was a World Cup champion, and nothing could take that away.

Remember, big dreams take time to achieve. Alex's World Cup victory was the result of years of hard work and determination. So keep practicing, keep believing, and who knows? Maybe one day you'll be lifting a World Cup trophy of your own!

CHAPTER 7: SUPER STRIKER: ALEX'S PLAYING STYLE

Have you ever wondered what makes Alex Morgan such an amazing soccer player? Let's dive into the skills and strategies that make her a super striker!

First things first: speed. Alex isn't called "Baby Horse" for nothing! When she sprints down the field, she's like a blur of red, white, and blue. Defenders often find themselves eating her dust as she races past them with the ball at her feet.

But Alex isn't just fast – she's quick too. What's the difference? Well, speed is how fast you can run in a straight line, but quickness is about how fast you can change direction. Alex can stop, start, and turn on a dime, leaving defenders spinning in circles!

One of Alex's secret weapons is her ability to read the game. It's like she has a soccer sixth sense! She can predict where the ball is going to be and gets there just in time to score. It's almost like magic, but really, it's the result of years of practice and studying the game.

Alex is also known for her powerful and accurate shots. Whether she's using her right foot, left foot, or even her head, she can send the ball flying into the net from almost anywhere on the field. She practices her shooting for hours, working on placing the ball in the corners where goalkeepers can't reach.

But being a great striker isn't just about scoring goals. Alex is a team player too. She's always looking for ways to set up her teammates to score. This is called an "assist," and Alex is just as happy assisting a goal as she is scoring one herself.

One of Alex's coolest moves is her ability to play with her back to the goal. This is really tricky because she can't see where the goal is! But Alex has practiced this so much that she knows exactly where to turn and shoot, often surprising the goalkeeper.

Off the field, Alex works hard to stay in top shape. She eats healthy foods, gets plenty of sleep, and spends lots of time in the gym. Being a world-class athlete isn't just about what you do during the game – it's a full-time job!

Alex is always trying to improve her game. She watches videos of her matches, looking for ways to get even better. She also studies other great players, both past and present, to learn new tricks and techniques.

But perhaps the most important part of Alex's playing style is her never-give-up attitude. Even if her team is losing or she's having a bad day, Alex always gives 100%. She believes that with hard work and determination, anything is possible.

So, the next time you watch Alex play, look out for her lightning speed, clever moves, and powerful shots. And remember, all these skills didn't happen overnight. They're the result of years of practice, dedication, and love for the game.

Who knows? Maybe by working on your own skills and developing your own playing style, you could become the next soccer superstar!

CHAPTER 8: MORE THAN JUST GOALS

Alex Morgan isn't just a soccer superstar on the field – she's a champion for important causes off the field too! In this chapter, we'll explore how Alex uses her fame to make a positive difference in the world.

One of the biggest issues Alex cares about is equality in sports. She noticed that sometimes, women's soccer teams don't get the same pay or recognition as men's teams. Instead of just accepting this, Alex decided to speak up! She and her teammates fought for equal pay and better working conditions. It wasn't always easy, but Alex knew it was important to stand up for what's right.

Alex is also passionate about helping kids stay healthy and active. She visits schools and community centers, encouraging young people to play sports and exercise. She even wrote a series of books called "The Kicks" about a young girl's soccer adventures, inspiring kids to follow their dreams both on and off the field.

But Alex's caring nature doesn't stop there. She's an ambassador for UNICEF, an organization that helps children around the world. Alex has traveled to different countries, using soccer as a way to connect with kids and bring attention to important issues like education and health care.

65

Alex also cares a lot about the environment. She's partnered with organizations that work to keep our oceans clean and protect wildlife. She often reminds her fans about the importance of recycling and reducing waste.

As a role model, Alex knows that many young fans look up to her. She uses her social media platforms to share positive messages about self-confidence, hard work, and kindness. She's not afraid to show her real self – including the challenges she faces – which helps her fans see that even superstars have ups and downs.

Alex has also used her voice to support other athletes. When gymnasts spoke up about abuse in their sport, Alex stood with them, showing that athletes from different sports can support each other.

Even with all her success, Alex never forgets where she came from. She often goes back to her hometown to host soccer clinics, giving local kids the chance to learn from a World Cup champion!

One of the coolest things about Alex is how she balances being a top athlete with other parts of her life. She's a mom, a businesswoman, and an advocate for causes she believes in. She shows that you can chase your dreams and still make time for the other important things in life.

Alex once said, "I feel it's my job to inspire the next generation." And that's exactly what she does – not just by scoring goals, but by showing how sports can be a powerful tool for positive change.

Remember, being a champion isn't just about winning trophies. It's also about using your talents to help others and make the world a better place. Just like Alex, you have the power to make a difference, both in your sport and in your community!

CHAPTER 9: THE JOURNEY CONTINUES

As we reach the final chapter of our story, you might think this is where Alex Morgan's journey ends. But guess what? For Alex, the adventure is far from over!

Even after winning Olympic gold and becoming a World Cup champion, Alex keeps pushing herself to new heights. She knows that in sports, just like in life, there's always room to grow and improve.

These days, you can find Alex playing for the San Diego Wave FC in the National Women's Soccer League (NWSL). It's a new challenge for her, helping to build up a brand new team and inspire soccer fans in a different city. Alex approaches this challenge with the same enthusiasm she had as a rookie on the national team.

But Alex's goals extend far beyond the soccer field. She's become a powerful voice for women in sports, fighting for equal pay and better opportunities. She wants to make sure that the young girls who look up to her will have even more chances to shine when it's their turn to take the field.

Alex is also tackling the challenge of balancing her career with being a mom. She gave birth to her daughter, Charlie, in 2020, and quickly returned to playing at the highest level. She hopes to show other athlete moms that it's possible to chase your dreams and be a parent at the same time.

Looking to the future, Alex has her sights set on more big tournaments. There are more World Cups to win and Olympic medals to chase. But for Alex, it's not just about adding to her trophy collection. It's about continuing to inspire people around the world and show what's possible when you work hard and believe in yourself.

Alex also dreams of a day when women's soccer is just as popular and well-supported as men's soccer. She's working hard to grow the game, not just in the United States, but globally. Who knows? Maybe one day we'll see professional women's soccer leagues in every country, with packed stadiums and millions of fans!

As she moves forward in her career, Alex is also thinking about her legacy. She wants to be remembered not just as a great soccer player, but as someone who made the sport better for future generations. She's mentoring young players, supporting grassroots soccer programs, and using her voice to make positive changes in the game she loves.

For all the young dreamers out there, Alex has a message: "Your journey is your own. Don't be afraid to work hard, to speak up for what you believe in, and to dream big. The path might not always be easy, but it's always worth it."

As we close this book, remember that Alex Morgan's story is still being written. And in many ways, your story is just beginning. What amazing chapters will you write in your life? What goals will you score, on and off the field?

Remember, every great journey starts with a single step. Alex's journey began in her backyard in Diamond Bar. Where will yours begin?

So, lace up your shoes, chase your dreams, and who knows? Maybe one day, someone will be reading a book about your incredible journey!

CONCLUSION

Wow! What an incredible journey we've been on with Alex Morgan, from a little girl kicking a ball in her backyard to a world-renowned soccer superstar. Let's take a moment to reflect on the amazing adventure we've just read about.

We've seen how Alex's love for soccer started on the playground and grew into a passion that took her all the way to the World Cup and the

Olympics. We've cheered along with her as she scored winning goals, and we've learned how she faces challenges both on and off the field.

But Alex's story is about so much more than just soccer. It's about dreaming big and working hard to make those dreams come true. It's about never giving up, even when things get tough. And it's about using your talents to make the world a better place.

Remember how Alex stands up for what she believes in? How she fights for equality and inspires young athletes everywhere? That's just as important as all the goals she's scored.

As you close this book, think about your own dreams. Maybe you want to be a soccer star like Alex, or maybe your passion is for something completely different. Whatever it is, Alex's story shows us that with determination, practice, and belief in yourself, amazing things are possible.

Here are some lessons we can all learn from Alex:

1. Start where you are - Alex's journey began in her backyard.
2. Practice, practice, practice - even superstars have to work hard!
3. Be a team player - success is sweeter when shared.
4. Stand up for what's right - use your voice to make positive changes.

5. Keep learning and growing - there's always room for improvement.

6. Inspire others - your actions can motivate people around you.

So, what's your next chapter going to be? Whatever it is, remember Alex Morgan's spirit, determination, and kindness as you write your own story. Who knows? Maybe one day, you'll be inspiring others with your incredible journey!

Now, go out there and show the world what you can do. Your adventure is just beginning!

Quiz Time!!!

1. Where did Alex Morgan first fall in love with soccer?

   a) At school

   b) In her backyard

   c) At a professional stadium

   d) At the Olympics

2. What nickname did Alex's teammates give her because of her speed?

   a) Speedy Gonzales

   b) Lightning Bolt

c) Baby Horse

d) Rocket Girl

3. In which year did Alex Morgan win her first Olympic gold medal?

a) 2008

b) 2010

c) 2012

d) 2015

4. What is the name of the book series Alex wrote to inspire young soccer players?

a) The Goals

b) The Kicks

c) The Wins

d) The Stars

5. Which organization did Alex become an ambassador for, helping children around the world?

a) FIFA

b) UNICEF

c) WHO

d) UNESCO

6. What important cause has Alex fought for in women's soccer?

a) Longer seasons

b) More teams

c) Equal pay

d) Bigger stadiums

Answers:

1. b) In her backyard

2. c) Baby Horse

3. c) 2012

4. b) The Kicks

5. b) UNICEF

6. c) Equal pay

Made in the USA
Las Vegas, NV
06 February 2025